A PR Practitioner's Guide to Activist Groups

When and How to Respond

KEVA SILVERSMITH

Would that you give as much energy to your
dreams as you do to your fears
—Unknown

CONTENTS

INTRODUCTION

An old public relations hand once told me: "Crises are just a part of doing business." Unfortunately for businesses, they aren't built to handle crises. Even brilliant business minds are often caught flatfooted by bad publicity, and get confounded in particular by public protests and activist group demands.

When I lecture on anti-brand activism, I start off my presentation by explaining that I have no personal position related to the examples that follow. I have been paid by for-profit entities to argue their points of view, but I'm certain that activists have legitimate grievances.

In any event, my dispassion is just good practice. If you get swept up in the emotion and politics of the groups attacking your company, you'll put at risk your personal credibility and your company's reputation. Your company will lose customers, and in the end you'll still give in to the activist group's demands.

As examples of group activism, I share three news stories I pulled from a Google search almost at random.

The headline of the first, dateline San Diego, reads: "PETA stages chalk protest in front of La Jolla restaurant." The gist of the article is that People for the Ethical Treatment of Animals wants the California Pizza Kitchen to have its cheese suppliers phase out the de-horning of their dairy cows. If you follow the topic through to the PETA website, you'll find Casey Affleck starring in a disturbing two-minute video about the practice, and right below, the email address of the California Pizza Kitchen CEO.

The second article I highlight is from Palo Alto, California, headline: "Protesters target Apple's labor practices." The article begins:

> Apple is in the crosshairs because critics want it to improve working conditions in China where Apple products are assembled.

During a global day of action against Apple, these protesters delivered signed petitions to company retail stores on both coasts and at some international locations. Store employees in New York City were no doubt rattled by the band of journalists who descended on the store "in a mess of camera flashes and waving microphones."[1]

---

[1] Bonnington, Cristina and Carter, Beth. "Protesters Crash Apple Stores, Demand Apple 'Manufacture Different.'" *WIRED*, 9 Feb 2012. Web. 11 March 2014.

My third example shows a picture of the White House with a throng pressed between the Lafayette Square grass and the White House's wrought iron gates. One protester is holding a sign sketched with a skull and crossbones that says: "MONSANTO HOME of GMOS & AGENT ORANGE." The headline of the story says: "Monsanto Video Revolt: Global anti-GMO online rally launches."

* * *

When a well-organized activist group shows up asking for money, a change in company policy, or a shift in the way the company conducts business, the group knows your company is likely unprepared. Activist group pressure occurs so far outside the normal course of business that few executives possess any firsthand experience.

Furthermore, activist demands and tactics offer up to executives a new intellectual challenge. Many executives, accustomed to their power within their organizations, buoyed by their professional success, and familiar with outthinking their competitors, begin to relish the chance to tangle with activists. When attacked personally, executives instinctively retaliate. And besides, there's often a degree of ego involved when an executive is confronted by Occupy Wall Street types.

The problem for the company is that all this emotion, energy and intensity is terribly misdirected. You're running full speed into the activist group's trap.

1 THE ANATOMY OF AN ACTIVIST GROUP ATTACK

The diagram on the next page shows the kinds of tactics an activist group will use to get your company to submit to its demands. I drew up this chart based on my own observations, but activist groups are very sophisticated and work from thick manuals. Activist groups will roll out these kinds of tactics until executives feel a level of pain they can no longer tolerate – and finally agree to make changes.

Although activists focus a great deal of attention on the C-suite itself, you should note how everything in this chart trickles down to the corporate communications department at the bottom right. Hassled executives, flustered customer service agents and media outlets of all types come calling on beleaguered public relations people for answers.

The Activist Group Playbook

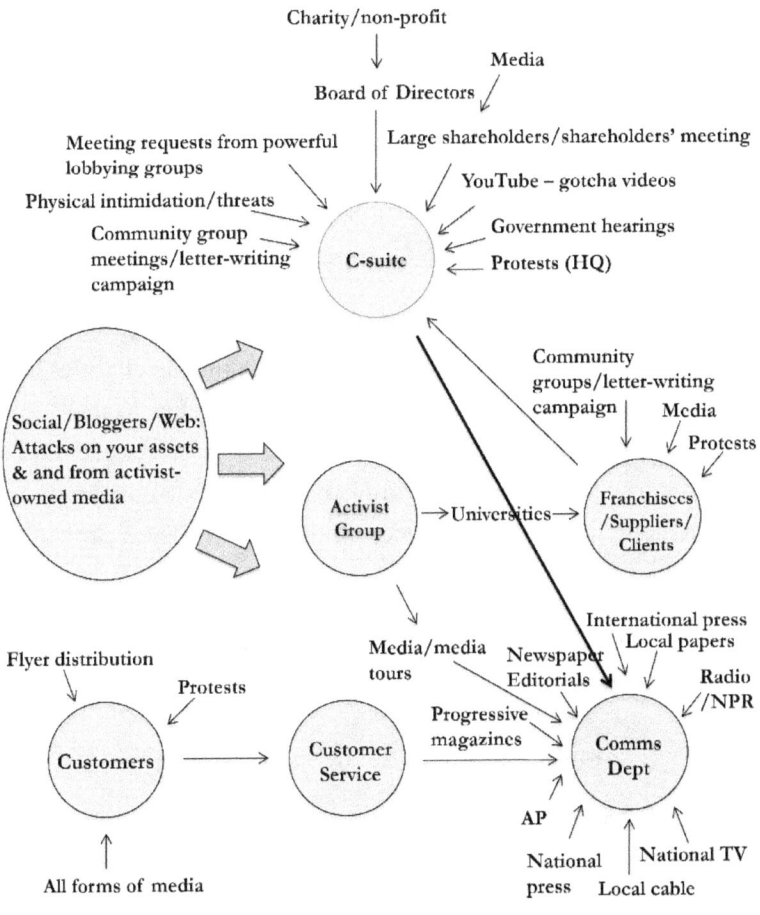

The C-suite attack

Activists excel at sowing discord within organizations. While the C-suite may initially be united in their opposition to activist demands, activist groups are masterful at breaking through. Once the CEO starts to disagree with the legal department which is at odds with the VP of operations who is arguing with marketing, the game is over. This kind of internal friction is a waste of energy and simply bad business.

Charities/non-profits

Activists know they can get to the C-suite through the company's board of directors. While rank-and-file employees answer to the C-suite, the C-suite answers to the board. And the board of directors answers to their spouses.

Many board member spouses sit on high-profile charities and other non-profits. Activist groups with close ties to these non-profits use their connections to hound the spouse: Did you know that your significant other oversees a corporation whose behavior is in conflict with the very mission of this organization?!?

The spouse brings the activism home; phone calls get made, emails start to fly.

Media

It's unimportant whether an overarching left-wing media bias actually exists. It is important to understand that when activists gear up to take on a business, a squad of journalists stands ready to activate with them. In many cases, these journalists are closely affiliated with the activist group as members, advisors and contributors.

One creative way the media gets to the C-suite is by badgering large shareholders and private equity groups that have a stake in the company. These players, many of whom sit on the company board of directors, often oversee multiple – if not dozens – of other investments. Rest assured, they have no interest in the details of some activist group controversy at one of their portfolio companies. These investors will demand to know from the C-suite why this minor issue is being handled so poorly that the press is calling *them* for comment. It's actually quite embarrassing.

YouTube gotcha videos

Once you've engaged with an activist group, sending your executives out in public takes on a whole new level of risk. That plum keynote address you secured for your CEO at the annual chamber of commerce meeting? It ends with your CEO striding off stage and stepping into an activist's smartphone camera ambush. Your CEO's stammering, fumbling, impromptu response to the activist's accusation is captured for all eternity. It is posted on the activist group's website, emailed out to the group's database, and shared with thousands on social media.

Government hearings

Some of the hearing rooms for the United States Congress are quite exquisite. They are cathedral-like spaces that must be modeled after the interior of some European palace. There are magnificent, towering marble pillars that hold up fantastically ornate molding, with spectacular chandeliers illuminating the rich wood paneling and lush carpeting that runs the length of the hall. And best of all, your CEO will get to see it! Activist groups have sympathizers in high places. Members of Congress will hold hearings and sometimes subpoena your leadership in order to apply additional pressure.

Physical intimidation/threats

I've heard some apocryphal stories related to companies in disputes with unions. The CEO starts noticing the same black sedan with tinted windows showing up at his daughter's soccer games and other family outings – never explicitly threatening, but always menacing.

Recently, activists have started crossing the public/private line more aggressively. In January 2014, it was reported that:

> A protest group calling itself Counterforce on Tuesday demonstrated in front of the Berkeley, Calif., home of Google engineer Anthony Levandowski and distributed leaflets to his neighbors to bring attention to "the evil he brings into this world" through involvement in technology projects ...[2]

Google has begun hiring security guards to protect its employees.

---

[2] Claburn, Thomas. "Stop Harassing Google Employees." *InformationWeek*, 25 Jan 2014. Web. 27 Feb 2014.

Meeting requests from powerful lobbying groups
Letter writing campaigns
Headquarters protests

With the goal of increasing executive pain, activist groups will engage with allies to generate unrelenting pressure. Your CEO will get meeting requests from celebrity activists, social justice advocates, church groups, and movement leaders. Letters to the CEO will pour in, filling boxes around the office. Activists might even stage a protest at your company's headquarters, and refuse to leave until they meet with a member of the C-suite.

Your distracted leadership will start spending a substantial amount of time just dealing with the activist group, to the exclusion of running the company. This disruption of the business is entirely intentional, an underlying strategy of activist tactics.

Franchisees/Suppliers/Clients

Activists will target individuals and businesses that serve your company in a supporting role. If your associated businesses have connections to universities, expect student groups to get involved as well.

While activism is a challenge for your team at headquarters, your franchisees and suppliers are often small, privately owned operations with absolutely no capacity to handle protests, media inquiries and letter writing campaigns. Just think of the hapless employees in Apple's New York store confronted by a media gaggle, a professional activist, and "a woman dressed in an iPod costume."[3] In cases like this, local

9

employees are possibly frightened, certainly unprepared, and with cameras rolling, you've got a completely uncontrolled public relations event on your hands.

These attacks threaten relationships between your company and key contacts, who may decide it's just easier to do business with someone else. These attacks are also disruptive because the owners of these small businesses will be on the phone with your C-suite constantly, imploring them to MAKE IT STOP.

Consumers

If your business sells direct to consumers, expect activists to try and create some financial pain as well. Your customers will be confronted by protests at retail locations, and they will find activists passing out defamatory flyers in communities all around your sales area. In addition, your customers will be on the receiving end of all kinds of provocative media, whether it's an article they read in the newspaper or something they see on Facebook.

As a result of these efforts, your customer service department will be bombarded by calls and emails asking for an explanation.

Communications Department

The press calling continually for interviews about the activist story is not open to persuasion. They are not interested in your opinion, commentary or argument. In fact, their story is already written, and they are seeking a quote simply to

---

[3] Bonnington, Cristina and Carter, Beth, Op Cit.

enhance the flow of their article. In many cases, the reporter is hoping that you (or an executive) misspeak, so they can highlight your poorly phrased quote in their article.

I recommend responding to all activism-related press inquiries with a carefully worded email statement. There is no point in providing anything more.

Web and social media

Only imagination limits an activist group's ability to destroy the reputation of an individual or company through the web. In fact, governments have been ruminating on this very issue, studying techniques and writing documents about how to ruin people online. Here are some suggested tactics:

> "[F]alse flag operations" (posting material to the internet and falsely attributing it to someone else), fake victim blog posts (pretending to be a victim of the individual whose reputation they want to destroy), and posting "negative information" on various forums.[4]

At a minimum, activist groups will clog up your brand's Facebook page, leave a thread of nasty comments on every tweet, and share like crazy the earned media written by their allies in the press.

---

[4] Greenwald, Glenn. "How Covert Agents Infiltrate the Internet to Manipulate, Deceive, and Destroy Reputations." *The Intercept*, 24 Feb 2014. Web. 26 Feb 2014.

* * *

If your company is under attack by an activist group, let me suggest one thing: Just settle. Activists are engaged in asymmetrical warfare, and you can't win regardless of the outcome. You are in the business of making widgets, and anything that disrupts that focus must stop.

I can think of only two cases when it makes sense to fight.

2 WHEN TO FIGHT

Resisting the demands of professional activists is such a destructive experience that I would counsel against it in all circumstances but two.

When you are the founder/owner of the business

When a company's CEO is also its founder, every aspect of the business becomes personal. Though the founder's sensitivity will be exploited, he or she may determine that the issue is a matter of integrity. He won't tolerate dissent from anyone, particularly some outside organization telling him how to run his business.

When an activist group's demands pose an existential threat to the business

Sometimes activists make demands that are incompatible with a company's business model. Examples include environmentalists trying to stop a developer's construction project, animal rights groups opposing a company's use of animals, and naturalists objecting to a technology company's technology. In these cases, the business has no choice but to fight for its survival.

Which groups should you take seriously?

While activist groups of all sizes are capable of inflicting damage, some groups start with more resources than others. The largest activist groups are multinational NGOs with balance sheets, organizational charts and brand valuations that rival global corporations. A direct confrontation with an organization like Greenpeace, Amnesty International or WWF is basically unthinkable; however, a new book by two professors called *Protest Inc.: The Corporatization of Activism*, suggests that activist NGOs have also become sensitive to image. These transnational entities are prioritizing easily measurable outcomes in order to demonstrate a "return on donations," rather than supporting incendiary activist tactics.[5]

As a result, the world's largest corporations are joining with NGOs to form mutually beneficial partnerships. Companies are incorporating NGO affiliations into their marketing to boost their reputations as good corporate citizens; NGOs get access to corporate boardrooms, but also generate a new stream of revenue. By way of example, WWF's partnership with Coca-Cola in 2010 was worth around $20 million.[6]

The next level of activist groups are mid-sized organizations, led by or receiving advice from career activists. These career

---

[5] Lebaron, Genevieve and Dauvergne, Peter. "Not just about the money: corporatization is weakening activism and empowering big business." *openDemocracy*, 14 March 2014. Web. 15 March 2014.

[6] *Ibid.*

activists have devoted their lives to refining tactics, expanding funding and building alliances. They spent their college years learning from the inventors of group activism, took internships with the pioneers of large-scale activism, and later organized their own 501(c)(3) organizations. Some mid-sized groups disguise their sophistication through a carefully cultivated appearance of grassroots action. Regardless, they are directed by senior professionals every bit as knowledgeable and skilled in their field as your executives are in yours.

Despite the prevalence of trained activists, you'll sometimes find yourself up against genuine amateurs. You'll also discover that executives can get very anxious about negative press, irrespective of the nature of the publisher and the size of its audience. A jumpy VP will occasionally present you with a printout from some obscure website or blog, seeking both reassurance and a solution. Early in my career, I would have said that stories from such trivial sources should definitely be ignored. Today, however, information spreads so fast, and media attention is so unpredictable, that you must take everything seriously.

The curious case of the African Rain Tree

One of the key features of Fort Lauderdale, Florida, is the New River. This waterway enables boaters with inland waterfront homes to sail out to the ocean, and provides striking views for restaurant guests and condo residents along its route.

The African Rain Tree, Fort Lauderdale, Florida.

A firm named Cymbal Development expressed a desire to build a residential tower on a vacant lot overlooking a small section of the river. If you visit the lot, you'll see (behind the chain link fence) a mature tree with a wide canopy topped off with some fairly light foliage. This lumbering specimen is called an African Rain Tree, possibly one of the largest in North America. Cymbal Development put forth a site plan that moved the tree to a safer, more prominent location on the property, and promptly drew the wrath of some local environmentalists and a scattering of regional media.

In March 2013, the Fort Lauderdale-based *Sun Sentinel* ran an article titled, "Rain tree supporter fired over YouTube video." The article begins:

> Until last week, Chris Brennan was in good
> favor as senior first mate for the Water Taxi

… Now he's unemployed. Brennan was fired two weeks ago for shooting YouTube video about a developer's plans to move a giant rain tree in Fort Lauderdale. … In Brennan's case, his bosses told him his advocacy was at odds with the Water Taxi business. Water Taxi leases its hub from the developer who wants to move the gigantic tree: Asi Cymbal, and his company, Cymbal Development. Cymbal saw the rain tree video and, when he found out it was shot by a Water Taxi employee, called Brennan's boss.

News about the firing became a hot local story and even a national sensation: the story appeared one morning on the news ticker of NBC's *Today Show*. Incredibly, the story of a municipal zoning dispute related to a tree ultimately ended up being broadcast to a national audience of hundreds of thousands.

You must take everything seriously.

3 HOW TO FIGHT

Activists want you to engage them in a very contentious and public dispute. Your engagement through whatever corporate channels you choose – a post to your tens of thousands of social media followers, a prominent explanation on your high traffic website, your outreach to friendly journalists – lets the activist group hijack your communications machine. Unwittingly, you generate awareness for the activist group orders of magnitude greater than what they could have accomplished alone.

Moreover, your attention gives the activist group credibility and power. The high profile corporate entity you represent has identified this organization as worthy of attention; you have elevated the activist group from obscurity while your defensiveness has diminished your own brand.

Some could argue that irrespective of your company's response, sympathetic journalists will help an activist group reach a critical mass of publicity. I would suggest that the disruption taking place in the newspaper industry is undercutting traditional activist tactics. When newspapers downsize and their audiences shrink, activists and their allies lose some ability to wreak havoc through established channels.

On the other hand, social media now gives each person and each organization the chance to be their own media publisher and media company. Corporations and their leaders can be hit from every direction.

It is an axiom among activists that corporations don't bleed, but people do. An attack against some corporate trademark will gain little traction, but embarrass an individual and you'll get that person's attention very quickly. Over the course of an activist group's campaign, company leaders should expect to be called out by name publicly and criticized personally. And thanks to social media, the heckler isn't silenced just because he's escorted out of the room.

Activists seek to not only maximize executive pain, but also to provoke a mistake. Many executives have unintentionally revived a stalled activist campaign by pushing back too hard. Viewed this way, the story of the African Rain Tree is a demonstration of more than unpredictable mainstream media coverage. It is also lesson about how the reaction to activism can itself generate unwanted exposure and attention.

Blackfish and SeaWorld

Blackfish is a documentary that takes an unflattering look at the treatment of animals by marine parks, with a particular focus on a killer whale's fatal attack on a SeaWorld trainer. A week before the film's release in July 2013, SeaWorld and its public relations firm sent a detailed, 8-point analysis of the movie to 50 film critics prior to their screenings.

The makers of *Blackfish* could not have dreamed of a more contentious and public dispute. *Blackfish* gleefully posted on its website a flashing yellow banner that said "SeaWorld REACTS" – and linked to their own detailed rebuttal of SeaWorld's denial. Though the public probably had little awareness of the film's release, SeaWorld's response became a blockbuster news story:

New York Times: "SeaWorld's unusual retort to a critical documentary"
ABC News: "SeaWorld Calls 'Blackfish' Documentary 'Inaccurate, Misleading'"
Business Week: "SeaWorld fights back at the critical documentary 'Blackfish'"
MSN: "SeaWorld upset about 'Blackfish' film's portrayal of their orca whale"

Committed to denouncing *Blackfish*, SeaWorld continued on with its own counter-campaign. The company has paid to publish an open letter from SeaWorld's animal advocates in major newspapers, added content to its website about SeaWorld's expert animal care, and launched paid social media campaigns to highlight its recently produced educational videos.

The press, delighted by the flow of fresh story angles, dutifully checks in with the *Blackfish* filmmakers for comment after every new SeaWorld assertion. Following the playbook perfectly, the *Blackfish* team responds for comment by issuing lengthy statements; they also recently challenged SeaWorld to a public debate.[7]

---

[7] Kaufman, Amy. "'Blackfish' director on Oscar snub, SeaWorld's new PR

In reality, the content of SeaWorld's educational offensive may be 100 percent accurate. *Blackfish* may be "propaganda," as it says on SeaWorld's website. There may be little truth to the "allegations made by animal extremist groups" as SeaWorld told the *Orlando Sentinel.*[8] However, SeaWorld is drawing battle lines, and the public is being forced to choose sides.

How to fight: Neutralize the conflict

Activists crave a very contentious and public dispute. While the degree of public is somewhat out of your control, you can very much dictate the amount of contentiousness and the amount of dispute.

Your message in every dynamic – whether it's your CEO being ambushed at a speaking engagement, your emailed response to press, or the statement you've drafted for customer service – is: We care, we agree, and we are delighted to work together to come up with the best solution. In meetings with church groups and movement leaders, your only question is: "How can we help?" We are all on the same side and we all want to achieve the same goal.

If all parties appear to be working together, the activists' agitation is drained of its purpose. The media will get bored and ignore it, and your customers will lose interest and forget about it.

---

offensive." *Los Angeles Times,* 21 Jan. 2014. Web. 4 March 2014.

[8] Connolly, Kevin P. "SeaWorld concert: Heart drops out after Barenaked Ladies, Willie Nelson ditch Orlando festival." *Orlando Sentinel,* 7 Dec. 2013. Web. 8 March 2014.

In a similar fashion, you can slow down an activist group by pressing for specificity around their vision for change. Activist groups are very good at making general, sweeping demands, but rarely have they developed a detailed method of implementation. This posture is partially strategic, placing the pressure for action on the corporation; on the other hand, it reflects an activist group's lack of insight into business operations. When applicable, you can wear away at an activist group's credibility by seeking their technical input and insisting on a resolution that includes their meaningful contribution.

4 SOCIAL MEDIA CONSIDERATIONS

The principles for managing activism on your social media properties are the same as in the physical world: responding to your critics gives them legitimacy. You risk elevating your adversary and diminishing yourself. Likewise, while you can't control the hostility on activist blogs and social media pages, you choose the response to the attacks taking place on yours.

There are many excellent articles online that explain the importance of setting community guidelines for your social media properties and providing a clear commenting policy. You should feel free in your guidelines to ban personal attacks, profanity and the like. Once you have your comment policy in place, you can delete inappropriate posts with confidence.

On the other hand, your policies don't inoculate you against legitimate objections and concerns. When an activist campaign has you in its sights, you should be prepared for a surge of criticism on your online platforms.

Give your detractors a voice

The dialogue made possible by social media creates an additional challenge around optics. Your company comments behind the logo of a billion-dollar, multinational brand, which can come crashing down on the brave, solitary advocate for social justice. In our culture predisposed to favor the underdog, a careless social media response can quickly turn your adversary into a victim, rallying more popular support.

The best practices for community-building on social media are especially important when it comes to activism. You should redouble your commitment to honesty and transparency if you choose to respond to an activist group. For example, shutting down a heated conversation maximizes the appearance of conflict. However, by engaging activists in civilized discussion, you end up disarming your critics in the general public. Moreover, this new frame helps you build trust among the "lurkers" who are watching how you respond before making up their minds.

Furthermore, by engaging with your detractors, you have an opportunity to correct misinformation and blatant misrepresentations. Your calm and composed alternate point of view gives you the chance to win over your audience and to build your own community of advocates.

Finally, this honest and open discussion positions your brand as a credible source. You become a trusted outlet for information related to the activist group's demands.

Successful community self-policing

A robust community of advocates is the most powerful force in social media. A positive grassroots response from your followers is a strong validation of your position, an authentic reaction that is much stronger than your brand's public relations spin.

When I managed the Census Bureau's social media outreach during the 2010 Census, the agency faced a great deal of hostility related to issues of privacy and government intrusion. In spite of the 2010 Census' ten simple questions, one woman in particular posted her objections relentlessly on our Facebook page. She believed that the survey asked questions well beyond what private citizens should be forced to divulge, or would ever supply voluntarily.

Someone in our Facebook community decided to do a little research about this woman. With a simple name search on Google, this advocate was able to quickly locate and provide virtually all the information our relentless poster needed for her 2010 questionnaire – age, address and race. With her ignorance exposed, our relentless poster suddenly disappeared.

Sometimes, however, your community of advocates will be unable to respond effectively. In the case of the census, one individual critical of the program demanded answers related to the agency's marketing budget. Although our community told him his concerns were unfounded, he refused to give up until we provided him with the specifics he requested. We had to provide the answer in order to make him stop.

A note about Facebook

While a Facebook page filled with nastiness might seem unsightly to you, it's important to remember that the vast majority of your Facebook fans never see these posts. Every fan visits your page once – to Like it – and then reads about your brand only when you publish a post that appears in their news stream. You as the community manager see every criticism and attack, but you need to keep in mind how your fans interact with your page.

Of course, everyone can see the comments added below each post. But, if your community guidelines forbid off-topic comments, you can go ahead and delete comments that are strictly disruptive and have nothing to do with the particular status update. Every so often you should post a reminder about your commenting policy to preempt accusations of censorship.

CONCLUSION

Blackfish may have become a national story regardless of SeaWorld's approach, lifted to prominence by airings on CNN, and the chance for an Academy Award nomination. SeaWorld's best shot to set the record straight might have been to accept the filmmakers' offer to appear on camera during the creation of the documentary. Hindsight being 20/20, SeaWorld's decision to accept *Blackfish*'s offer would have been an example of "take everything seriously." (If a SeaWorld spokesperson had consented to an on-camera interview, the company would have needed to roll its own recording equipment alongside *Blackfish*'s as a deterrent against being misquoted.)

Perhaps the best answer in SeaWorld's case would have been to rely on the old-fashioned tenets of crisis communications.

Your top priority as a crisis communicator is to get your company's bad news out of the headlines and to stop the hashtag from trending on Twitter. This "Headline Strategy" approach to crisis communications means your brand absorbs one news cycle of bad coverage – the initial surge you can't prevent, but you take the right steps to stop the story there. Success with the Headline Strategy requires that you offer up full transparency to the press and public.

Your legal department will resist this strategy, wanting to release as little information as possible due to fear of liability. The problem with crisis management by smokescreen, however, is that journalists (and online troublemakers) are professional investigators – if they sense you are covering up pieces of the story, they will continue to dig. And they will write about the crisis, cycle after cycle, as they tunnel down to the truth.

The formula for full transparency is a time-tested crisis paradigm. You tell the public:

1) What you know
2) How you're going to fix it
3) Why you should be trusted to fix it

Trust is the hardest part, of course, and why reputation management is really a year-round endeavor. Every enterprise knows its public relations weaknesses – in SeaWorld's case, concern over the treatment of animals. Your communications campaign around your continuous improvement in your vulnerable areas lays the foundation for your successful crisis response. While the activist press might already have its story written, you at least have the opportunity to neutralize the general public – your customers – and get ahead of reputational threats to your business.

As part of its *Blackfish*-related social media campaign, SeaWorld published a tweet in January 2014 that said: "Hear the real SeaWorld story from trainers past and present. Don't be misled by activist hype [link]." The tweet received hundreds of replies, lots of them negative. I was reminded of a quote attributed to Mark Twain, that "a lie can travel halfway around the world while the truth is still putting on its shoes." One pithy reply stuck out to me, expressing the feelings of many, and capturing the essence of SeaWorld's public relations challenge:

"@SeaWorld nobody believes you."

ABOUT THE AUTHOR

Keva Silversmith is an accomplished public relations professional with deep, hands-on experience across the spectrum of communications roles and tactics. He has worked as a lead communicator in the private sector, in government and in the non-profit world. Educated as an attorney, Keva brings strategic insight to reputation management and crisis communications.